Original title:
Cherry Blossom Chorus

Author: Nora Sinclair
ISBN HARDBACK: 978-1-80566-760-5
ISBN PAPERBACK: 978-1-80566-830-5

Blossoms in a Sea of Air

Flowers are giggling in the breeze,
Dancing around with such foolish ease.
Pollen sneezes, oh what a sight,
Bumbling bees get lost in delight.

A butterfly slips, lands on a hat,
The wearer stares like, "What’s up with that?"
Petals tumble, a pink-laden storm,
Who knew spring could be so... warm?

Dance of the Soft Pink Clouds

Up in the trees, a ruckus brews,
Like fluffy clouds in bright pink hues.
Squirrels prance with a cheeky grin,
As the blossoms whirl, let the chaos begin!

A bird trips over a branch with flair,
Feathers fluffed in a stylish air.
Everyone's laughing, oh what a day,
In this wild garden, we dance and sway!

A Symphony of Sweetness

In the orchard, humor takes flight,
With fruity notes that spark pure delight.
A bumblebee sings out of tune,
While flowers join in, a whimsical croon.

Lemonade spritzers spill in the sun,
As giggles resound, oh isn’t this fun?
With petals afloat, it’s a jolly brawl,
Nature's concert, we’re having a ball!

Whirling Petals at Dusk

As dusk arrives, a playful charm,
Petals swirl round, causing no harm.
An awkward dog does a spin and a flop,
While children with laughter can’t seem to stop.

A cat jumps high, trying to catch,
The flying fluff in a hilarious match.
Under the stars, the laughter roars,
With petal confetti, who could ask for more?

The Gathering of Blooming Spirits

In the park, a mishap blooms,
A squirrel steals my tasty plums.
Birds giggle at my failed snack,
While petals rain like sweet, pink flak.

Laughter dances on the breeze,
A tumbling dog, a sneezy tease.
Blossoms twirl in playful flight,
As we joke through the soft sunlight.

Bikes go wobbly, kids take a spill,
We laugh until our cheeks turn ill.
A kite gets stuck in a tree's embrace,
All we can do is burst out in grace.

In this gathering, joy is found,
With chuckles and smiles all around.
Spirits bloom, we're on a roll,
In swirling chaos, we find our soul.

Gentle Spills of Color

Petals tumble, what a sight,
Like candy tossed from a kite.
We race beneath a vibrant sky,
And dodge the blooms as they comply.

A picnic spread of silly snacks,
Balloons that wiggle, tumble, relax.
Orange slices land on my nose,
While everyone laughs, and nobody knows.

A chair collapses, laughter swells,
As someone yells, 'Hey, who smells?'
We point at the sweets now smeared,
Amid the giggles, none are jeered.

The meadow hums a bright tune,
While bees cartwheel under the moon.
Gentle spills of color dance,
And in this mess, we take a chance.

Inhaling Spring's Essence

With noses up, we stroll and sniff,
What's that smell? A giant whiff!
Is it flowers or someone's lunch?
We all lean in, it's quite the crunch.

A dog barks loudly, wags his tail,
Chasing blooms like a holy grail.
We trip over roots, oh what a sight,
And laugh till dusk replaces light.

Goblins, giggles—crazy dreams,
As laughter bursts like silly streams.
Just one inhale, oh what a tease,
A sneeze escapes, brings us to knees.

Inhaling spring, we melt away,
With every gust, more games to play.
Laughter fills the fragrant air,
Creating fun without a care.

The Echo of Leafy Dreams

Chasing shadows, we dart and weave,
With every twist, we laugh and believe.
Petals tremble under our feet,
As we skip like dancers, oh so sweet.

The echo of giggles fills the space,
Softly stirred by spring's embrace.
A misstep sends a friend to the ground,
We fall beside them—laughter's our sound.

Twirling hats and dancing shoes,
In this kaleidoscope, we choose.
A leaf flutters down like a hat,
And who knew it'd land on that?

In leafy dreams, we find our bliss,
A cascade of fun, we cannot miss.
So join us here for the ride,
In this joyful trip, we all abide.

Nature’s Tender Symphony

In gardens bright, where colors clash,
The bees hold meetings, oh what a bash!
With buzzing tunes and pollen dance,
They wear those stripes as if by chance.

While flowers giggle and sway around,
A snail in shades of lime is found.
He’s stuck on grass, but dreams of flight,
And debates with ants 'til it’s night.

In the Shadow of Pink

Underneath the blooms so grand,
A squirrel juggles with great command.
He drops a nut — oh, what a mess!
The birds just laugh, their wings impress.

A floating leaf gives all it’s got,
It spins and twirls, like it’s in a pot.
The wind just giggles, can't take it slow,
With nature’s humor in full flow.

Enchanted Petal Rain

As petals fall, the dance begins,
A puppy leaps, but he just spins.
He catches one and gives a bark,
While snails just watch, in the dark.

A group of frogs starts quite a show,
Their croaks in chorus, a funny flow.
They try to sing and hit the high,
But all we hear is an off-key cry.

The Song of Fragility

A butterfly flaps with all its might,
While ants march round like it's a fright.
"Excuse us, madam!" they fuss and moan,
With bits of crumbs they claim as own.

The sun peeks out, its selfies gleam,
Flowers pose, living the dream.
But wind shows up, what cheeky blow!
A petal lands right on a toe!

Beneath Canopies of Silk

Underneath pink puffs, we giggle and sway,
The petals rain down, oh what a display!
A breeze steals our hats, oh, look at them fly,
Who knew nature's pranks would make us so spry?

The air's filled with laughter, a sweet little tease,
Squirrel sneaks a snack, doing acrobat ease.
With every soft rustle, the fun never ends,
Birds join the chorus, we need no amends.

Echoes of the Season's Kiss

Giggles bounce high, as petal ships sail,
We dodge and we dive, in a jovial trail.
Each bloom's a soft lollipop, pink, round, and neat,
Who knew springtime sweetness could tickle our feet?

The wind plays a tune, it's a zesty affair,
While ants dance around, without a single care.
We laugh at their hustle; they've got it all wrong,
Why work so hard when life can be song?

Nature’s Blushing Melody

In gardens of laughter, we twirl and we trip,
A dance with the petals, a fanciful skip.
Each flower’s a wink, it catches our sight,
And soon, we’re all twirling, a colorful sight!

The bees join the party, with buzzing so bold,
“Join in!” they invite, their antics are gold.
We stumble and fumble, it’s terribly fun,
Who knew being clumsy could be so well done?

Fluttering Petal Overture

Amidst a big swirl of soft blush and glee,
We chase down the petals like kids on a spree.
A hat on a girl, a shoe on a tree,
Invisible strings pull us to jubilee!

The breeze is a jester, a whirlwind of cheer,
Sprinkling pink laughter, we're all in the clear.
In this vibrant concert, we’re dancers and jesters,
Who knew spring could be such fun little testers!

Fragments of a Sunlit Wish

The petals dance in the breeze,
Like giggling kids on their knees.
They swirl around, a pink delight,
Dodging bees in a frantic flight.

A squirrel steals some from the ground,
Wearing them like a crown, proud.
Nature's whimsy, a wild jest,
As laughter fills the sunlit zest.

With every bloom comes a new joke,
Like how the trees play hide and poke.
The grass whispers secrets so grand,
As blooms wink from a merry band.

So tip your hat to the silly sprout,
With every petal, there's no doubt.
Nature's humor spreads all around,
In a vibrant world that can't be found.

The Ballet of Welcoming Colors

Colors twirl in a brilliant show,
For flowers to flaunt and bestow.
They pirouette on a breeze's cue,
Leaving us giggling at all they do.

Daffodils take a comical stance,
While daisies join in for a dance.
Petals twinkle like stars on the ground,
In this funny ballet, joy abounds.

The sun, a spotlight, beams down bright,
As flowers perform their hilarious flight.
With faces painted in cheeky hues,
Each bloom's a character with quirky views.

A rabbit hops in with a bow,
"Look at me! I'm the star! Wow!"
With laughter ringing from the green,
The stage of spring is truly seen.

Tenderness in Blooming Free

The flowers whisper soft and low,
In a giggle, they steal the show.
Embracing the sun with open hearts,
Uncle Sun sends them silly darts.

Bumblebees buzz with a goofy grin,
As blossoms wave their petals thin.
They tease the wind with little spins,
Gathering joy as the fun begins.

A wily fox peeks from behind,
With a chuckle, he's feeling kind.
“Can’t catch me, I’m faster than you!”
Flowers giggle as they bloom anew.

With each laugh that the petals share,
Springtime pranks fill the sunlit air.
A comedy played on nature’s stage,
Tender moments that never age.

Poetic Unfolding of Springtime

As spring arrives, the pranks commence,
A floral feast, a teasing tense.
Petals giggle as they unfurl,
Inviting whimsy to dance and twirl.

The ants march in with a parade,
Tiny soldiers, unafraid.
With funny hats made of green leaves,
Together they weave through blooming thieves.

A butterfly plays a game of tag,
Wings like ribbons, not a drag.
The flowers cheer as they flit and fly,
In this light-hearted, springtime sky.

So raise a glass to the blooming cheer,
With every laugh, let’s draw near.
Nature's humor, a playful sight,
In the unfolding of pure delight.

The Melancholy of Blooming Days

When flowers giggle in the breeze,
They tease the bees with sneezy wheezes.
A petal falls and starts to spin,
"Stop that, you silly! You'll get a grin!"

The trees are dressed in pink delight,
Prancing about, oh what a sight!
A squirrel slips, does a ballet twist,
As blossoms dance in a springtime mist.

Birds join in with a chorus loud,
Singing praises, drawing a crowd.
But watch your head, it's quite a mess,
With love notes dropped from plants in dress.

So raise a cup to fleeting blooms,
A toast to laughter in the rooms.
For when they fade, we’ll hold our breath,
And wait for more—each giggle’s theft.

Flutters of the Awakening Dawn

At dawn, the flowers start to tease,
With little giggles flapping with ease.
They sipped the dew and spilled the fun,
Said, "Who needs sleep? Let’s all be done!"

A chubby bee, he sips and sways,
Buzzing loudly through the brightening rays.
He’s got a dance, flamboyant and bold,
Twirling petals, feeling quite controlled!

The sun peeks in with a cheeky grin,
As blossoms chuckle from deep within.
'Tis a party, oh what a delight,
Demure petals in raucous flight.

So come and join this jocund spree,
Where even daisies sing with glee.
We’ll flaunt the joy till daylight’s end,
And watch the flowers as they blend.

Swirls of Farewell Colors

The petals flutter, a vibrant show,
As colors spin in a silly flow.
"Goodbye, old friends!" they shout with cheer,
With confetti laughs, they disappear!

A gust of wind brings mischief bright,
Spinning blossoms, oh what a sight!
They swirl around like hats gone mad,
Creating mayhem, oh so glad!

“Catch me if you can!” calls a hue,
While petals giggle in the morning dew.
But watch out, my friend, they’re quite the tease,
They’ll stick to your nose like tiny fleas!

So say farewell to the blooming spree,
For colors swirl with jubilee.
Dance with the winds, embrace the day,
As laughter fades, but it’s here to stay.

The Call of the Garden Spirits

In gardens deep, where giggles hide,
Mischief blooms with petals as their guide.
They whisper secrets, soft and bright,
While critters join the jolly light.

With raucous voices, the fae appear,
Tickling flowers, full of cheer.
“Join us now, and let’s create,
A whirlwind of joy, oh isn't it great?”

Bees paint patterns in the air,
While butterflies flounce without a care.
“Spin us tales of the night and day,
As blossoms giggle, come join the fray!”

So heed the call of spirits fair,
In every bloom, there's laughter to share.
For in this garden, fun never dies,
In colors that dance and tease the skies.

Petals in the Spring Breeze

Petals float and spin away,
Like confetti in the play,
Squirrels dance on branches high,
While birds sing and aim to fly.

The sun peeks through, a golden glare,
It tickles noses in the air,
Grasshoppers join the funky jam,
And ants march by, “Oh, look, a ham!”

When sneezes echo through the park,
A thrilled dog gives a playful bark,
“Bless you!” says a lady near,
As pollen makes the laughter clear.

So let’s rejoice in spring’s embrace,
With quirky prances, funny grace,
Under blooms that giggle too,
Springtime’s jest is made for you!

Whispers of the Blooming Trees

Leaves chatter secrets on the breeze,
While bees hum tunes with total ease,
A squirrel slips on a grassy slope,
"Someone save me!" shouts the hope.

Buds giggle as they start to show,
Getting bashful, moving slow,
With each warm day they swell and tease,
"Oh please, don't peek! We are just trees!"

Underneath, a picnic's laid,
Sandwiches and dreams displayed,
A lady drops her fruity drink,
"Let's toast to spring, and not to stink!"

So join the fun beneath the trees,
With whispered laughs carried by the breeze,
Nature's jesters dressed in pink,
Life's a laugh - don't you think?

Ethereal Serenade of Pink

In a garden where laughter sways,
Each flower nudges in playful ways,
Frogs in tuxedos croak their tune,
While bumblebees juggle under the moon.

Colors splash like paint from a brush,
Buds burst open in a happy rush,
The sun wears shades, oh so chic,
While daisies giggle at the peak.

A cat's tail twitches in delight,
Chasing petals that take to flight,
“Catch me if you can!” they tease,
While grass tickles the overseer’s knees.

Oh, the joy that springtime brings,
With bubbling laughter and fluttering wings,
Join the merry, silly spree,
As flowers dance, so wild and free!

Dance of the Fragile Blooms

Tiny blooms on tipsy stems,
Waltz together like silly gems,
A ladybug leads the grand parade,
With laughter echoing through the glade.

Pollen floats like glitter bright,
As butterflies take wondrous flight,
A sneezing fit disrupts the groove,
"Excuse me, spring! Let's make a move!"

Amid the blooms, a picnic spread,
Scones and jams, just like I said,
"Watch the crumbs, the ants will cheer,"
As tiny feasts could draw them near.

So sway along with petals' grace,
In nature's funny, joyful space,
With laughter twinkling all around,
In this dance where joys abound!

Fragrance of the Tender Dawn

In early light, we hear a joke,
A flower sneezed, and then it spoke.
"I'm just so bright, I can't contain!"
The bees all laughed, and lost their gain.

With petals swirling in the breeze,
The ants all dance, they're here to tease.
They dress in outfits far too grand,
Then tumble down—oh dear! They planned.

The morning hums with silly cheer,
A raccoon waves, it's time for beer!
The sun peeks in with a playful grin,
As blooms all blush beneath their skin.

So raise a cup, and toast the dawn,
To flowers bright and squirrels drawn.
With laughter echoing through the trees,
Let's sing of fun until we sneeze!

Timeless Whispers

Old trees gossip like best friends,
About the owls and their weekend bends.
They chuckle as the squirrels conspire,
To steal some nuts, or find a choir.

A dandelion tells a tale,
Of when it danced upon the rail.
"I twirled and spun, and then I fell!"
The daisies giggle, "Oh, do tell!"

A birduit called from high above,
"Let's all unite and spread the love!"
With wings outstretched, they flapped away,
And landed quickly—what a play!

They sing of spring, a funny mess,
With nature's charms, it's hard to guess.
In every breeze, a secret known,
A timeless joke that's always grown!

Sweet Symphony of the Season

Look here, a bunny with a hat,
It hops along—what's up with that?
He conducts the flowers with a bow,
They sway and giggle, 'Is that how?'

The birds all chirp a silly tune,
While squirrels bop beneath the moon.
The daisies dance in fuzzy shoes,
Each petal nods to share the news.

A hedgehog smiles, he’s found a pie,
He takes a nibble and starts to cry.
"It’s raspberry jam, oh how divine!"
And suddenly it’s dessert-time!

So join the laugh, let’s spread delight,
Among the blooms, oh what a sight!
In every petal, joy we find,
A symphony that’s sweet and kind!

Walk Among the Blossoms

Come take a stroll among the blooms,
Watch out for bees and their funny fumes.
They buzz around like they're on cue,
With tiny hats and shades of blue.

A butterfly winks, it's quite the show,
It twirls and flutters to and fro.
The tulips tease, they boast about,
Who can stand straighter, without a doubt.

The sun displays its golden glow,
As giggles pop like corn, you know.
A ladybug trips, it spins in place,
Then rolls away with oops! That face!

So laugh and skip, let spirits rise,
Amid the petals, hear the sighs.
A joyful jaunt, with nature's grace,
A walk among the blooms, embrace!

A Symphony of Floral Dreams

In a park where petals fly,
A bird tried to eat one, oh my!
It thought it was a tasty treat,
But ended up in quite the feat.

A squirrel danced with such delight,
While dodging blooms in morning light.
He twirled around an unseen foe,
A ladybug dressed all in yellow.

The bees, they buzzed a silly tune,
As flowers bloomed beneath the moon.
They argued 'bout the best bouquet,
While flowers laughed, ‘We’re here to stay!’

A snail watched with a lazy cheer,
Declaring springtime, “Oh my dear!”
He missed the fun, but smiled and thought,
“Awareness is what I just forgot!”

Soft Hues in a Quiet Dawn

At dawn they wake with sleepy sighs,
In pajamas made of petal dyes.
A wind that sings, oh so discreet,
While flowers laugh, "What a treat!"

The cat, in awe, tried to catch them,
But tripped over a sprightly stem.
"Oh my!" the daisies all exclaimed,
"Is that our feline friend? How famed!"

The rabbits hopped with joy in tune,
With little hats made from the moon.
They held a dance, the quiet kind,
While sunbeams winked and laughed behind.

A ladybug brought snacks to share,
But the ants arrived and caused a scare.
"Line up! Line up!" the lady cried,
As chaos reigned, they laughed and sighed!

Blooming Ballet Beneath the Sky

The flowers twirled, a merry sight,
In costumes bright, they danced with might.
A grasshopper joined, with leaps so grand,
He shouted, “This is my land!”

A petal floated down with grace,
And landed right on Mr. Ace.
He swatted it away, but who knew,
It was his hat for the dance debut!

The daisies formed a conga line,
While tulips shouted, “Ain’t this fine?”
A butterfly swirled, lost in his groove,
Buzzing along, so hard to move.

The sky turned pink, a stage so bright,
As flowers danced till the fall of night.
And when the moon peeked from above,
They all agreed, they felt the love!

The Language of Fragility

In the garden, whispers spread,
"Hurry! Don't step on that!" they said.
A gentle breeze, a shiver near,
"Careful now, we hold each dear!"

A gnome sat, offering tea,
To petals drifting carelessly.
"Come sip with me," he said with glee,
"Swing low, it's a fragile spree!"

A tree complained of pesky pranks,
As squirrels climbed and vied for ranks.
"Stop shaking me!" it grumbled low,
While flowers giggled; "Oh, take it slow!"

And when the sun began to set,
They planned a party, no regret.
"Let's toast to life!" they cheerfully cried,
In a world where whimsy won't subside.

Echoes of Floral Renewal

Petals swirl like confetti, oh what a sight!
Bees buzzing like a band, playing all night.
Squirrels in tuxedos, dancing with flair,
While the flowers gossip, without a care.

A dog in a hat thinks he’s quite the star,
Chasing after bunnies, oh how bizarre!
Laughter fills the air, as friends gather round,
In this floral fiesta, joy knows no bound.

Every breeze whispers secrets, oh so sweet,
Tickled by the sun, warming up our feet.
Blossoms giggle softly, it's a sight to see,
Nature's grand comedy, endlessly free.

A picnic spreads out, with snacks by the tree,
While ants in a line march in harmony.
Who knew spring laughter could bloom like this?
And dancing with petals brings moments of bliss.

Rhythm of Soft Hues

Bouncing butterflies have got the moves,
Grooving on petals, they shake and improve.
A caterpillar joins with a wiggled swing,
Making all the flowers laugh, it's a hilarious thing!

Colors collide in a playful parade,
Tulips wear sunglasses, looking half-jaded.
Daisies are gossiping, sharing some tea,
A riot of laughter in blooms full of glee.

The wind plays a tune, a silly soft breeze,
Making trees dance awkwardly, with such ease.
While the babies giggle, as pups chase their tails,
In a whirl of colors, joy never fails.

Even the clouds join in, fluffing their hair,
While raindrops play drums, a tune beyond compare.
In this soft canvas where laughter is king,
Every vibrant chuckle makes the seasons sing.

Meeting Under Pink Canopies

Under canopies lush, where laughter's aglow,
A picnic ensues, as the sun starts to show.
Friends play charades with a sandwich in hand,
While ants crash the party, not planned but quite grand.

Silly hats on heads, shaped like a flower,
Baking up jokes, we laugh and devour.
A frog leaps in rhythm, a dance of delight,
Making us giggle until the sky's night.

The breeze tells a tale, of mishaps at noon,
When the cake took a tumble, oh, what a cartoon!
Candy melts in sunshine, a sticky surprise,
As everyone chortles, we savor the skies.

With petals falling down like a vibrant snow,
Life's absurdities make spirits grow.
Underneath these blooms, laughter's our reign,
In this playful haven, joy blooms again!

A Dance Amidst the Blossoms

In a swirl of petals, we find our parade,
With bees doing the cha-cha, they're unafraid.
The daisies are twirling, the roses, they sway,
As sunshine erupts in a light-hearted play.

A wiggly worm leads with a boogie-woogie,
While the bugs in the grass get a bit moody.
They trip over pollen as they join in the throng,
Nature's big dance-off, where all feel they belong.

With laughter like music, we sway side to side,
Unruly squirrels bounce, with nothing to hide.
A laugh and a twirl, a hop and a spin,
As springtime declares, let the fun now begin!

So, gather your friends, and choose a neat spot,
Where petals rain down, in a dance you can't plot.
Amidst all the blossoms, let's cherish the cheer,
In this wild floral festival, laughter is near.

Tapestry of Transience

Petals fall like confetti, oh what a scene,
The trees throw a party, so fresh and so green.
Bumblebees dance, with moves so absurd,
While squirrels hold meetings, to chit and be heard.

Wind whispers secrets, in a playful tone,
As the blossoms all giggle, not wanting to moan.
A ladybug winks, as she struts on a leaf,
While the grass gets jealous, feeling such grief.

Laughter erupts when the rain starts to play,
Droplets become marbles, they roll as they sway.
The daisies join in with their bright, sunny cheers,
While the tulips keep gossiping all through the years.

What a sight to behold, this transient parade,
Life blooms like a joke, never to fade.
Let the petals keep falling, let the laughter abound,
In a tapestry woven, joy all around.

Secrets in the Softest Light

In the softest of shades, where whispers convene,
Tiny ants plan their heist, but they're rarely seen.
A butterfly flutters, on the hunt for a snack,
While shadows of clouds form a gossamer track.

The bees pull a prank on a snoozing old cat,
Who dreams of a mouse that was never a spat.
While daisies giggle, their heads bobbing low,
They remind every passerby, 'We've got the show!'

The sunlight sneaks in, just to tickle the thyme,
A raucous performance, quite silly, yet sublime.
Petals perched on noses, they dance out of tune,
As laughter erupts with the rise of the moon.

In this realm where the odd meets a daydream delight,
Every bloom shares a chuckle, a shimmer, a sight.
So keep your secrets close, under the soft light,
For there's plenty of laughter when flowers unite.

Harmony Wrapped in Bloom

In a garden of humor, where smiles interlace,
Blossoms chatter cheerfully, holding their space.
A tulip teases a daffodil bold,
'What’s with that trumpet? You think you’re so gold?'

The bumblebees whisper, in sweet harmony,
'We buzz while we work, so come dance with me!'
A hedgehog retreats, from a swirl of confetti,
He grumbles, 'This party's too loud and unsteady!'

Petals pirouette, on a breeze that’s a hoot,
While grasshoppers sing, in their tune so astute.
The sun spills its laughter, fills every crevice,
As blooming antics unfold, with joyful finesse.

Wrapping up the day, in blankets of cheer,
Nature's own symphony rings sweet in your ear.
With every soft rustle, and giggle in bloom,
Life's funny and fragrant, dispelling all gloom.

Reverie of the Elusive Spring

Oh what a delight, when the season comes round,
With jests in the breeze, and soft giggles abound.
The flowers conspire, in a colorful quest,
While frogs croak the tunes, putting humor to test.

A rabbit in slippers hops right out of a hat,
'Hey there!' he yells, 'Mind if I join in the chat?'
The petals explode with a burst of good cheer,
As the sun shoots confetti, the party is here!

Dancing on sidewalks, the folks muddle through,
With flower crowns donned, and faces all blue.
Their antics are silly, as they trip and they twirl,
Creating a canvas, with laughter to swirl.

Amidst all the blooms, comes a twist of surprise,
As nature’s own jester, begins to arise.
So cherish the folly, as spring flutters in,
With joyous reverie, let the funny begin!

Serenade of Spring

In the park where laughter's found,
Petals dance upon the ground.
Squirrels chase with silly glee,
While birds join in a tuneful spree.

Sunshine tickles, it's no jest,
Pollens swirl, a nasal fest.
Old folks sneeze, oh what a scene,
As blossoms burst like confetti green.

Breezes whisper playful tales,
Of tiny shoes and little trails.
A dog prances, chasing tails,
In the bloom where joy prevails.

So we dance like fools today,
In splashes pink, we laugh and sway.
With every giggle, petals fly,
Spring's comedy beneath the sky.

Fragile Dreams in Bloom

A kite tangled in a tree,
Sways gently, what a sight to see!
Kids below laugh and shout,
What will come of this stout bout?

Bumblebees in suits so dapper,
Buzz around, making us clapper.
Their little dance, oh what a feat,
Forgetting pollen in the heat.

Old man tugs at his grandkid's sleeve,
"Do you feel the magic weave?"
She giggles hard, all in good fun,
He ticks her nose, "It's a pranking run!"

In this realm of floral cheer,
Laughter fills the atmosphere.
With every bloom, a grin appears,
A silly symphony for all ears.

Beneath the Pink Canopy

Underneath this pinkish glow,
Gnomes and fairies put on a show.
A cat creeps in, all quiet and sly,
Pouncing on petals that flutter by.

With each flurry of joyous shock,
Someone drops their ice cream block.
Kids shriek loud, their giggles swell,
As whipped cream flies to say 'Oh well!'

Above, a crow starts to caw,
While dressed in blossoms—what a flaw!
It struts and boasts of fancy dress,
Confused, it leaves us in the mess.

Beneath this canopy, who could tell?
Springtime laughter casts a spell.
Fools and jesters, let us cheer,
Life’s a prank when spring is near.

Elysian Melodies

In the garden, where we sway,
Buds erupt in bright array.
A snail moves at his own pace,
While children race around the space.

With pink hats and goofy grins,
They tickle each other, that's how it begins.
A rogue breeze sends fliers up high,
As giggling blooms drift ever nigh.

Old women sip their tea with grace,
While bees buzz around the place.
"Mind the hat!" one shouts with glee,
As blossoms drift, a joyous spree.

The melodies of spring resound,
In playful antics all around.
With every chuckle, life's unrolled,
In hues of pink, we break the mold.

Songs of Renewal

In springtime's dance, we frolic and sway,
Silly squirrels join in, hip-hips hooray!
Pollen sneezes cause a laughter spree,
Flowers chuckle, 'Hey, look at me!'

The sun shines bright like a disco ball,
Butterflies twirl, having a ball!
Each bloom with a giggle, each petal a grin,
Nature's comedy, let the fun begin!

Bumblebees buzzing with a tune so sweet,
Hey, watch your head! Here comes a bee fleet!
They bumble and stumble, what a silly sight,
Dancing through the garden, oh what a light!

Fresh blooms agree, let’s keep it light,
With a wink and a nod, we set the night.
In every petal, joy kicked up a notch,
The world bursts forth, let’s dance and botch!

Petal-Paved Pathways

Down the lane where petals quilt,
I tripped and fell, oh what a jilt!
A flower laughed, 'Well, quite the spill!'
Nature's giggles, pure and shrill.

Each step I take, I slide with flair,
Twisting and twirling, rich in air.
Grass tickles feet, just can't resist,
A prancing frolic like I'm on a list!

Daisies gossip with gentle tease,
'Did you see that tumble? Oh, what a freeze!'
A breeze whispers jokes as it tickles my nose,
While sunlit giggles dance through the prose.

Hopping along this petal-paved way,
Remember, laughter makes the best play.
So join me now in this silly spree,
Life's more fun when you just be free!

Lullaby of the Blooming Hearts

Swirling petals in the moonlit night,
Little critters form a wobbly sight.
A ladybug hummed a lullaby,
While snoring frogs croaked, oh my, oh my!

The blooms all yawn, stretching wide,
With sleepy grins, they bend and slide.
A tulip whispers, 'Hush, it’s time for peace,'
But laughter erupts, never will it cease!

Stars snicker softly, twinkling in jest,
Nature's tunes put the world to rest.
But what’s this? A bunny hops away,
In pajamas, with flowers in disarray!

All the buds giggle, embracing the night,
As crickets play songs, a truly funny sight.
So close your eyes, dream a world anew,
Where laughter blooms in every hue!

Mosaic of Nature’s Grace

With colors splashed like a painter’s dream,
Nature giggles, ‘Oh, what a scheme!’
Grass blades giggle as they twist and bend,
Creating a canvas where fun doesn’t end.

Bumbling bees in a hilarious chase,
Chasing their tails in a dizzying race.
The blossoms clap, a comical cheer,
Nature’s concert, come lend an ear!

Oh, how the petals in springtime sway,
Dancing in rhythm, come laugh and play.
With each little twitch, the world finds its grace,
In this mosaic, life’s a funny place!

So grab your friends, let the laughter overflow,
In every corner, joy starts to glow.
Celebrate the whimsies, sing through the days,
In this funny mosaic, we all find our ways!

Transient Beauty Unveiled

Petals fall like clumsy cats,
Dancing off the boughs with splats.
A waltz of pink in air so bright,
They twirl and spin in pure delight.

Squirrels pause in cheeky glee,
As blooms rain down, 'Come play with me!'
They scamper 'neath the flower's shower,
Not caring much for time or hour.

A sneeze from me, oh what a sight!
The blossoms drift, taking flight.
I laugh and chase, arms swinging wide,
In this joyous, silly ride.

Spring's a jester, costumes grand,
Petal hats, and flowers planned.
With giggles mixing with the breeze,
Life's a dance—come bloom with ease!

Beneath the Blossom's Veil

A pink parade, so bold, so bright,
Underneath it, every sprite.
Fairies giggle, hiding there,
In between the petals' flair.

Bumblebees buzz, making sound,
As they flit and float around.
“Excuse me, sir!” one bee declared,
“Your flowers seem a bit unprepared!”

A dog runs by, attempting grace,
Chasing blooms in this wild race.
He leaps and trips, what a fine show,
As petals swirl, oh what a glow!

In this garden, joy does not fail,
Laughter reigns, beneath the veil.
So come and join, don’t be subdued,
For springtime’s fun is all renewed!

The Gentle Pulse of Spring

The day awakes with sunlit cheer,
As blossoms appear, oh dear!
Birds chirp tunes with funky flair,
In this vibrant, flowery lair.

A laugh erupts—what do we hear?
A cat is caught in blossoms near.
She pounces, trips, then shakes her head,
With petals tangled in her spread.

The buds whisper in playful tease,
"Life is short, take moments, please!"
Forget the stress, let worries slide,
In springtime's fun, let's now abide.

With every bloom, a new surprise,
Joyful moments, filled with sighs.
It's folly, sweetness, brightly sprung,
Come dance where laughter's sweetly sung!

Fluttering Whispers in the Breeze

Whispers float on gentle days,
As petals drift in playful ways.
We chase the blooms, as laughter grows,
In this game of blooming prose.

A pigeon struts, all puffed and proud,
Amidst the petals, it's quite loud.
"Watch me dance!" it seems to say,
While blooming joys come out to play.

A child spins, arms all a-flail,
"Look, Mom, look!"—a joyous tale.
The blossoms giggle, swirl around,
Creating giggles that resound.

As dusk draws near, with colors bright,
The breeze hums soft, a sweet delight.
Life's a festival in bloom's embrace,
With laughter, love, and cheerful space!

Lullaby of the Wistful Breeze

In the park, a squirrel prances,
Hiding nuts in secret glances,
While a grumpy cat on lawn,
Sneezes loudly, daydreams gone.

Petals dance like playful sprites,
Whispering secrets, sharing flights,
As a dog with joyful barks,
Chases shadows, plays in parks.

A kid with ice cream, oh so bright,
Wipes it clean, what a sight!
Tangled hair in breeze's tease,
Laughing hard, he takes at ease.

So let the world just twirl and spin,
With silly giggles from within,
For when the breeze begins to play,
Laughter greets the sunny day.

Timeless Elegance in Pink

Waving pink flags on a tree,
Nature's laughter, can't you see?
Old folks trying not to slip,
While holding on to their ice cream dip.

Silly birds in bowties sing,
In chirpy tunes, they sway and swing,
One forgets the words and squawks,
As the other two dance in solid block.

Passersby in striking hats,
Attempt to dodge the playful spats,
Stuck in hair, a petal tease,
They laugh and greet with such great ease.

As spring arrives with pranks galore,
Who knew nature could be such a chore?
In pink attire, the world ensues,
With giggles and jests that we all choose.

The Ephemeral Song of Nature

A blossom falls and hits my head,
Then hops away, like it's misled,
I chase it down with all my might,
Only to trip and lose my sight.

A robin sings, “Come dance with me,”
While I try my best to flee,
The pollen in the air does tease,
I’m the one who sneezes, if you please!

The sun dips low, then it will rise,
Awakening laughter, to no surprise,
Frisbees flying in careless glee,
Nature’s song, we sing so free.

So grab your friends and share a laugh,
Nature’s comedy, a silly craft,
While petals swirl like snowflakes bright,
Join the fun, from morn till night.

Caressed by Petals' Whisper

Petals whisper in the breeze,
Tickling noses, if you please,
A bee buzzes, wears a frown,
Can't remember where he's flown.

Children giggle, chasing dreams,
In the fields of blooms, it seems,
A puppy rolls with joyful yelps,
Dodging petals, silly elves.

Golden sun winks from above,
Nature's funny little love,
While grandpa dances with the air,
A twirl, a trip, without a care.

So as the day comes to a close,
With laughter held in every pose,
Let's toast to blooms that make us bright,
And all the joy, our hearts ignite.

The Colors of a Soft Goodbye

The petals dance, a comical flight,
They twirl and spin—oh, what a sight!
With sneezes and giggles, they swirl around,
A symphony of colors, absurdity found.

In the breeze, they play peek-a-boo,
Like shy kids playing, what do they do?
They scatter and group, in a merry parade,
Who knew springtime could be so mislaid?

A fluffy pink cap on a passing dog,
The trees chuckle soft, like a sweet fog.
With each little gust, they send out a cheer,
A riotous farewell as spring draws near.

So let's raise a toast to this fancy display,
The comedy of blossoms, in their own silken way.
For each fading petal holds laughter inside,
In this playful ballet, our grins can't hide!

Glimpse of the Fleeting Florets

Oh, look at the show! They scoff and they tease,
Pink whispers of spring ride the tickling breeze.
With a wink and a nod, the petals are sly,
In the game of the wind, it's all a big lie!

A cluster ups and dashes past cows,
Can you see them laugh? Take a deeper look now!
They whisper sweet secrets, just floating away,
In this goofy ballet, they're here for a play.

When blooming is done, and giggles all fade,
The leaves' giggly shouts, under moonlight cascade.
As we bid adieu, with a comedic flair,
Their whimsical essence lingers midair.

So gather around, as the flowers retire,
The tales of the goofy are what we admire.
For in every crinkle and loop-de-loop spin,
Fleeting moments remind us where laughter has been!

Tides of Spring's Romance

Oh the love in the air, with petals afloat,
A clumsy romance on a whimsy boat!
Two blossoms collide, like ships in a storm,
Spilling sweet nectar, in each flowery form.

They play a game of “catch me if you can,”
Fluttering flirtations, each little bud's plan.
A bee swoops in—oh, how rude, such a guest!
In this tangled affair, who can plead for rest?

The trees shake their heads at this flower-drawn mess,
While chatter and laughter grow louder, no less.
From laugh to a sigh, springtime dances near,
As petals crash wildly, we toast with good cheer.

So raise your glass high to this springtime crush,
With all its odd antics—oh, what a rush!
In nature's blender, where giggles collide,
Romance is silly, but we take it in stride!

Whispers Beneath the Sky

Beneath the grand blue, the petals conspire,
As they whisper sweet nothings, their giggles won't tire.
Like chatty old grannies with stories to tell,
They bounce on the breezes, under spring's spell.

With hats made of bloom and shoes spun of air,
They gossip and chuckle, without a care.
The sun beams down, quipping bright rays,
As laughter erupts in this fun-filled maze.

Now, the blossoms take turns in their feathery dance,
To each little whirl, they give spring a chance.
With hiccups of petals, they toss and they wave,
Each note of their laughter—a gift that they gave.

So if you look close, along the path you roam,
You'll see blooms chuckling as they start to comb.
For in every ripple that tickles the mind,
The essence of joy is what we all find!

Shimmering Petals in Melody

In the breeze they twirl and spin,
Dancing leaves with cheeky grins.
They giggle as they float away,
A jolly tune they love to play.

The bees hum off-key, buzzing loud,
While flowers sway, so very proud.
A raucous choir, the petals sing,
With all their joy, they let it swing.

Laughter ripples through the air,
As petals tease without a care.
They play hide-and-seek with the sun,
This floral prance is so much fun!

Oh, watch them tumble, round the park,
In shades of pink, they leave a mark.
With every gust, they leap and spin,
Springtime's giggles, they always win.

A Canvas of Springtime Serenades.

A canvas bright with merry sights,
Painted blooms in cheerful flights.
They wave at clouds that float on by,
As chirping birds begin to fly.

Each petal tells a silly tale,
Of squirrel pranks or a breezy gale.
They chuckle at the morning dew,
“Oh look, a puddle—time for a brew!”

With colors bold, they strut and sway,
Some shy, while others bold at play.
In this zany springtime show,
Every hue has room to glow.

The daisies dance with playful glee,
While tulips wink, “Come dance with me!”
In a joyful, swirling blend,
Each petal laughs, an endless trend.

Whispers of Petals

In soft whispers, petals tease,
They rustle secrets in the breeze.
A curious world, they spin around,
With hints of mischief all around.

Tickling each other in the sun,
A playful game has now begun.
"Oh look at that!" a daisy cries,
As butterflies flit past, oh my!

The petals laugh at grumpy trees,
"Oh lighten up!" they tease with ease.
With every drift, they share their cheer,
In nature's jest, the joy is clear.

From pink to white in tangled rows,
They bounce along where laughter flows.
Springtime's whimsy, bright and bold,
A joyous tale forever told.

Harmony in Pink

In harmony, they prance and sway,
Petals pink in bright array.
With quirky moves, they leap and spin,
Creating chaos, yet with a grin.

A goofy breeze comes for a snack,
And petals tumble, oh, what a hack!
They scatter laughter, rustle giggles,
As gardens burst with joyous wiggles.

The sun rolls in with a hearty laugh,
At silly blooms in nature's path.
They trip and tumble, what a scene!
Each petal born to be carefree and keen.

In clusters formed, they sing a song,
Of funny moments all day long.
A blooming band of springtime cheer,
With each fresh day, their joy's sincere.

Dance of the Fragile Wings

Petals twirl on a whisper of breeze,
Bumblebees dance with grace and ease.
Laughter floats like a feathered kite,
In a world where blossoms delight.

Squirrels pirouette, they flip and they flop,
Chasing each other, they hop and they stop.
Nature’s circus, the trees are the stage,
A leafy audience, wisdom of age.

Sunshine tickles, a warm, gentle tease,
Dandelions giggle, swaying with ease.
Every bloom and critter, a comic delight,
A springtime show, under soft, glowing light.

Springtime’s Gentle Lullaby

Crickets play tunes on a moonlit night,
Buds yawn and stretch, oh what a sight!
Ladybugs dream of sweet cherry dreams,
While the sun sneaks in with warm, golden beams.

Robins wear crowns made of blooming vines,
And caterpillars giggle, do silly signs.
The world spins softly in floral embrace,
As laughter fills every nook and space.

A parade of petals in comical flight,
Bouncing off clouds, oh what a delight!
With a whisper of spring, they twirl and glide,
In a playful waltz, side by side.

Ephemeral Elegance

Wings flutter softly, like secrets untold,
Dancing through gardens where laughter unfolds.
Grasshoppers leap, one tumbles and falls,
While the flowers chuckle at their funny brawls.

A breeze tells jokes, as daisies reply,
With giggles that scatter and float through the sky.
Colors explode, oh what a mess,
Nature's own canvas, we must confess!

Even the ants wear tiny, bright hats,
Attending the party with friendly chats.
In the arms of spring, like a theatrical show,
Every twig and bloom puts on a glow!

Voices of the Sakura

With every giggle, the blossoms proclaim,
Funny little stories, nature's own game.
Bugs in tuxedos, a dance on the breeze,
Whispering tales while climbing tall trees.

Frogs in their chorus, ribbit and croak,
While pondering life in a daffodil cloak.
They jump in unison, a froggy ballet,
Making the audience laugh all the way.

Petals drop down like confetti from cheer,
Celebrating spring, spreading love far and near.
With each tiny wink from the stars up above,
The night tells a joke, and blossoms laugh love.

Poetry in Pink

In a park where blossoms sway,
A squirrel steals a branch today.
He poses like a royal king,
While bees forget they couldn’t sing.

The flowers giggle in the breeze,
As birds strike silly poses with ease.
A picnic spread, but ants conspire,
To steal my sandwich, oh, they're dire!

Laughter rings where petals fall,
As people trip; they take a sprawl.
A dog chases after a kite,
It thinks it's a bird in flight!

Beneath the blooms, we dance and prance,
With every step, we take a chance.
Let’s join the fun, no time for gloom,
In the land where flowers bloom!

Serenade of the Awakening Season

Awake, awake, the world's a stage,
With blooms that turn a lively page.
A bashful bud peeks from its sleep,
And giggles softly, 'I won't keep!'

The sun pops up like morning toast,
While butterflies perform a boast.
They flaunt their colors in the sun,
A dance-off? Oh, this could be fun!

A ladybug wears polka dots,
While ants parade with tangled knots.
A breeze whispers a silly tune,
As flowers sway beneath the moon.

Each petal sways, a playful tease,
In this season filled with ease.
Come join the fun, no need to hide,
In the joy of nature, let's abide!

Petal-Scented Reverie

In the garden, chaos reigns,
Where petals fly in vibrant trains.
A clumsy bee steals nectar's prize,
While birds giggle at its disguise.

The trees shake hands, a secret pact,
They warn the blooms, 'It’s quite an act!'
Jesters of spring hop here and there,
With flower crowns, they comb their hair.

I tossed confetti made of bloom,
But squirrels thought it was their room.
They cheered and danced in bright delight,
While I just laughed at this wild sight!

So join the revel, lose your cares,
As nature plays with light affairs.
In this petal-scented spree,
Life’s a laugh, come join with me!

Chasing Spring’s Gentle Echo

A whisper calls from blooms so bright,
'Come dance with us, it’s pure delight!'
But as I spin, I trip and roll,
And land right in a flower's soul!

The trees all chuckle, leaves a-quake,
At this newcomer, oh, the mistake!
A ladybug sticks out its tongue,
As if to say, 'You’ve just begun!'

The world surrounds in every hue,
While rabbits join a hop or two.
They wink and blink, a funny sight,
As joy becomes a sheer delight.

So gather 'round this springtime cheer,
Where laughter reigns, and all's so dear.
With every step, a giggle flows,
In this game of springtime prose!

Swaying in Spring's Embrace

In the breeze, we dance with flair,
Laughing petals float through air.
Though we trip and tumble down,
Springtime giggles, not a frown.

Bees are buzzing, don't they know?
They join in on our little show.
With polka dots, they take the lead,
Together, we shall plant the seed.

The Veil of Delicate Colors

A pink parade is on the way,
Waving flags, we'll shout hooray!
Sippers spill their drinks with glee,
Oh, what joy, we're wild and free!

Windy whispers flirt with grace,
Chasing flowers, a silly race.
What's that hue? A ketchup stain?
At least our laughter is not vain!

Beneath the Petal-laden Sky

Underneath this floral dome,
We gawk at clouds, they look like foam.
A pigeon struts, he wears a crown,
In this madness, no one frowns.

As petals drift, we call a truce,
Rabid squirrels provide the juice.
A party's formed, oh what a blast,
Regretting no one’s past miscast!

An Aria of Fleeting Moments

Laughter rings through branches wide,
Each slip and slide brings us pride.
In the shade, we'll craft a tune,
With mock guitars we'll play till noon.

Moments whirl and twist about,
As giggles echo, there's no doubt.
A sneeze erupts, oh panic spreads!
Yet petals fall like soft deathbeds.

A Chorus of Spring's Awakening

The flowers nod with cheeky grins,
As squirrels dance on twirling fins.
Bee buzzes with a funky tune,
While frogs croak softly, 'We'll be here soon.'

A picnic spreads with treats galore,
But ants appear to start a war.
With sandwiches and lemonade,
We run to dodge the marching brigade!

The sun laughs down from skies so blue,
A kite takes flight, as if it knew.
A gust of wind, oh what a trip!
Our snack flies high, take a wild dip!

In laughter, spring comes jumping near,
With every bloom, a funny cheer.
In nature's theater, joy's in sight,
As everyone shares in pure delight.

Melodies of Barefoot Wanderings

With toes in grass, we stomp and shout,
As daisies giggle, round about.
A wriggly worm joins in the fun,
While sunbeams aim for everyone's run.

Our feet are dirty, oh so grand,
Painting rainbows on this land.
We twirl and leap in carefree glee,
As shadows join our quirky spree.

The trees tell tales, they sway and swing,
Their branches hum, 'Let's dance and sing!'
Silly hats on our heads so bright,
Transform us all into pure delight!

With flowers tangled in our hair,
We leap like frogs, no single care.
In every step, a joke unfolds,
Barefoot laughter, all ages hold!

Enchantment of Fading Light

As daylight wanes, the fireflies glow,
Their twinkling dance puts on a show.
A cricket strums his tiny string,
‘Join us,’ he chirps, ‘for evening spring!’

The sun bows down with a cheeky wink,
While shadows swirl and laugher links.
In twilight's glow, we chase the breeze,
While gentle whispers tease the trees.

We spot a cat, all poofed and proud,
Basking low beneath a cloud.
He stretches out and lets out a sigh,
“Spring’s too fun; you don’t even try!”

Our evening wears a golden crown,
As we giggle from dusk 'til down.
In fading light, our joy expands,
With nature’s quirks, we join hands!

The Poetry of Spring's Breath

With every breath, the flowers bloom,
Spreading laughter in the room.
A gust of wind with playful flair,
Leaves tickle noses everywhere!

A puppy bounds with bouncing cheer,
Sprinting towards the blooms so near.
He sniffs the air, then trips a bit,
Landing in the grass — a perfect fit!

The sky paints shades of cotton candy,
While butterflies dance — oh, so handy!
They flit and flutter with glee around,
In a world where joy is always found.

With every petal, a giggle plays,
As spring delivers its funny ways.
Let's bounce and sway, feel the mirth,
In this delightful time of birth!

Painting the Twilight Pink

As daylight fades, the skies blush bright,
A swirl of color in the fading light.
Dancing blooms with petals bold,
Whisper tales that never get old.

A squirrel tries to steal the show,
With blossoms perched atop its toe.
A gardener trips, a pot does fly,
Now there's a flower pot in the sky!

The painter grapples with his hue,
Fighting hard with shades of blue.
A canvas flees, he gives a chase,
While daisies giggle at the race!

Each tree's a wonder, each bough a jest,
Who knew that spring would be such a fest?
With blossoms laughing in the breeze,
Nature’s joke is sure to please!

In twilight pink, the world’s a show,
A circus of petals, on with the flow!
Each blush a giggle, each sigh a glee,
Oh, what a time to just let it be!

In the Heart of Renewal

Awake, awake, the blooms call cheer,
As bunnies hop, they quack, "My dear!"
Flowers splatter in pastel hues,
While bees buzz by, reciting news.

The tulips gossip as they sway,
About the daisies' awkward play.
A butterfly in a polka-dot suit,
Trips on a petal, falls on its boot!

The sunbreaks tease the buds to bloom,
While robins practice their finest tune.
And as the breeze makes blossoms whirl,
A daffodil plans to give twirls!

In gardens grand, the critters dance,
A sneaky squirrel swoops in for a chance.
Petals laugh and sing in time,
Nature's stage, the world a rhyme!

Oh, in renewal's heart we find,
The playful folly that nature's kind!
With every burst, there's mirth and cheer,
As blooms whisper, "Spring is here!"

The Secret Lives of Petals

There's a party beneath the trees,
Where petals chat and shake their knees.
With gossip sweet and stories grand,
They whisper secrets, oh, so planned!

A daisy swears to break the mold,
While roses share their tales of old.
A wind gust blows, and giggles spread,
As the blooms tumble, all cheeks red!

A bumblebee spins wild with grace,
Crashing into a shy geranium's face.
"Watch where you buzz!" the petunias shout,
"Oh, what a ruckus, what a clout!"

They all convene under the moon's light,
Sharing laughter through the night.
With every twinkling star above,
The petals bask in joy and love!

The petals live, they laugh and play,
In a curious bloom-fueled cabaret.
So next time you stroll and pass them by,
Know they're joyously throwing a sprightly high!

Notes of the Fading Day

As sun dips low, the night takes flight,
A serenade of colors bright.
The petals hum a lively tune,
As fireflies join, a dancing boon!

In the garden's heart, the crickets play,
Dancing shadows in soft ballet.
A potted plant takes a bow so deep,
While dreaming daisies drift to sleep.

One merry moth, an elegant flier,
Winks at blooms, a flirty liar.
"I'm the star of this nightlife show!"
But petals giggle, "Just so you know!"

In fading hues, the laughter blends,
Where petals sing and twilight bends.
With melodies that swirl and sway,
They welcome in the end of day.

So as you leave, hear their refrain,
The whispering blooms will call your name.
In every petal, a tune will play,
Notes of beauty in the dying day!

Harmony of the Spring Breeze

The wind is here, a playful tease,
It dances 'round like buzzing bees.
The trees wear pink, a giggling sight,
While petals drop, a confetti flight.

Kids chase them down, a race so grand,
With ice cream cones scooped by hand.
A flower fight breaks out with glee,
Oh watch out! Here comes Auntie Lee!

Laughter echoes in the air,
As blooms take flight without a care.
Nature chuckles, can't you hear?
Spring's silly songs are fine and clear.

So let's enjoy this wacky show,
Where all the silly winds can blow.
In the harmony, we find our way,
With giggles shared, we greet the day.

The Language of Petals

Petals whisper tales so sweet,
Of little squirrels with dancing feet.
They chat about the bees that hum,
And how they love a good, loud drum.

A sparrow joins, with a cheeky song,
It flirts with flowers all day long.
But who knew blooms could gossip so?
They spill secrets the breezes know.

"Do you see that guy with the green nose?"
They giggle on, as the garden glows.
The woodland critters roll their eyes,
While daffodils explode with sighs.

The sun sets low, but laughs remain,
As petals dance in a playful train.
Nature's chat, so witty and bright,
Brings joy to all in the fading light.

Embrace at Dusk

As dusk tiptoes on soft, pink feet,
The flowers hug the wind so sweet.
But wait, what’s that? A silly bee!
Trying to dance with a timid tree.

The branches sway in laughter's grip,
While shadows jive and petals skip.
“Hey, not too close!” a rose does shout,
As that bee twirls ‘round with no doubt.

The moon peeks in, a chuckling friend,
As twilight shows off its colorful blend.
Each bloom winks, a cheeky blush,
While fireflies join, adding to the hush.

Together they whirl in a twilight spree,
A party planned by Mother Glee.
In this embrace, with giggles bestowed,
Springtime ends on a joyful road.

Petals' Silent Serenade

Beneath the stars, the petals sigh,
With twinkling lights that fill the sky.
Yet listen close! What do we hear?
A silent tune that draws us near.

The moon laughs low, a quiet tease,
As flowers nod in the gentle breeze.
They sway in harmony, side to side,
While nature joins the midnight ride.

A fox trots by with a silly grin,
Whispering secrets of where he's been.
"Just grazing grass, it's quite the feast!"
The petals chuckle, "You're such a beast!"

With laughter wrapped around each stem,
The petals sing their secret gem.
In the stillness, joy cascades,
As springtime winks, in joyful parades.

www.ingramcontent.com/pod-product-compliance
Lightning Source LLC
Chambersburg PA
CBHW051628160426
43209CB00004B/561
9781805667605